A Note to Par

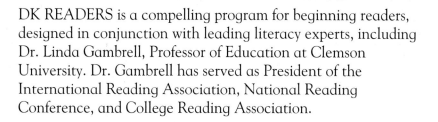

DK READERS is a compelling program for beginning readers, designed in conjunction with leading literacy experts, including Dr. Linda Gambrell, Professor of Education at Clemson University. Dr. Gambrell has served as President of the International Reading Association, National Reading Conference, and College Reading Association.

Beautiful illustrations and superb full-color photographs combine with engaging, easy-to-read stories and informational texts to offer a fresh approach to each subject in the series. Each DK READER is guaranteed to capture a child's interest while developing his or her reading skills, general knowledge, and love of reading.

The five levels of DK READERS are aimed at different reading abilities, enabling you to choose the books that are exactly right for your child:

Pre-level 1: Learning to read

Level 1: Beginning to read

Level 2: Beginning to read alone

Level 3: Reading alone

Level 4: Proficient readers

The "normal" age at which a child begins to read can be anywhere from three to eight years old. Adult participation through the lower levels is very helpful for providing encouragement, discussing storylines, and sounding out unfamiliar words.

No matter which level you select, you can be sure that you are helping your child learn to read, then read to learn!

LONDON, NEW YORK, MUNICH,
MELBOURNE, AND DELHI

For Dorling Kindersley
Project Editor Heather Scott
Designer Owen Bennett
Senior Designer Ron Stobbart
Brand Manager Lisa Lanzarini
Publishing Manager Simon Beecroft
Category Publisher Alex Allan
Production Controller Jen Lockwood
Production Editor Sean Daly

For Lucasfilm
Executive Editor Jonathan W. Rinzler
Art Director Troy Alders
Keeper of the Holocron Leland Chee
Director of Publishing Carol Roeder

Reading Consultant
Linda B. Gambrell, Ph.D.

First published in the United States in 2009 by
DK Publishing
375 Hudson Street
New York, New York, 10014

09 10 11 12 13 10 9 8 7 6 5 4 3 2 1
CD296—12/08

DK Books are available at special discounts when purchased in bulk for
sales promotions, premiums, fund-raising, or educational use.
For details, contact: DK Publishing Special Markets, 375 Hudson
Street, New York, New York 10014
SpecialSales@dk.com

Published in Great Britain by Dorling Kindersley Limited.

A catalog record for this book
is available from the Library of Congress.

ISBN: 978-0-7566-4528-1 (Hardcover)
ISBN: 978-0-7566-4527-4 (Paperback)

Color reproduction by Alta Image, UK
Printed and bound by L-Rex, China

Discover more at
www.dk.com
www.starwars.com

DK READERS

PROFICIENT
4
READERS

STAR WARS®

THE CLONE WARS™

Jedi Adventures

Written by Heather Scott

DK

Rising *Malevolence*

Plo Koon
Plo Koon is a
Kel Dor from
the planet
Dorin. In order
to survive on
oxygen-rich
worlds, Plo
Koon has
to wear
goggles and
a face mask.

The Separatists have a terrible
new weapon that has been
destroying Republic ships in
surprise attacks and leaving no
survivors. The Jedi Council decide to
send Plo Koon, a Jedi Master from
the planet Dorin, to the Abregado
system to hunt down this dangerous
new weapon before it strikes again.
Plo Koon leads three Jedi Cruisers
into the system, in his command
ship the *Triumphant*.

He spots a mysterious ship in the distance, silhouetted against a star.

The mysterious ship is the Separatist warship the *Malevolence*; Count Dooku and General Grievous are on board. A Battle Droid addresses them.

"We're tracking three Jedi Cruisers. What should we do?"

"Jam their transmissions," replies Count Dooku.

Malevolence
A Separatist warship, the *Malevolence* is General Grievous's prize flagship. It houses the Separatists' secret weapon.

Battle Droid
The Separatists' army is made up of Battle Droids. They are machines programmed to fight like soldiers.

Separatists
The Separatists oppose the Republic's rule and want to break away from its authority. They are made up of lots of different groups who want to rule themselves.

General Grievous
On his homeworld Kalee, Grievous was a warlord in his people's war against the Huk. He was transformed into a cyborg after a shuttle crash. He is a combination of a droid's body and his original brain, spine, and internal parts.

Plo Koon gazes out the window at the mysterious dark ship.

"I think it wise to report our position before we attack," Plo Koon decides.

"Skywalker's fleet is nearby, in the Bith system," replies clone Commander Wolffe.

"Good. Perhaps he can reinforce us," Plo Koon answers.

Plo Koon uses the HoloNet to contact Anakin Skywalker and his Padawan, Ahsoka, who are on the *Resolute,* a Jedi Cruiser.

"Koh-to-ya, Master Plo!"

"Koh-to-ya, little 'Soka," replies Plo Koon.

"How's the hunt for the mystery weapon going?" asks Anakin.

"We've tracked it to the Abregado system. We need reinforcements," Plo Koon replies.

"I'll have to ask the Council, Master Plo. I was given strict orders to protect our staging area," Anakin warns.

Suddenly Anakin and Ahsoka's holograms crackle and fade out. Plo realizes something is wrong.

Anakin and Ahsoka contact the Jedi Council over the HoloNet to ask for permission to help Plo Koon. Ahsoka is anxious that they get there quickly to help her old friend Plo Koon.

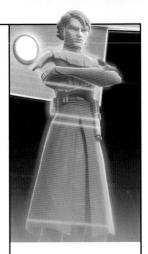

HoloNet
The HoloNet uses hologram technology to allow people to communicate instantly over vast distances.

Jedi Council
The Jedi Council is a group of the most experienced Jedi, who decide the course of action on important matters. Jedi such as Yoda, Mace Windu, and Plo Koon sit on the Council.

Plasma rotor
Plasma is a liquid that can transport things such as energy, and a rotor is a revolving part.

The enemy ship sets its targets on the Jedi ships.

"General Grievous, this will be a suitable test for our new weapon. You may fire when ready," Count Dooku says.

"Yes, my Lord," Grievous replies. The plasma rotor on the *Malevolence* begins to glow brighter. White-hot energy sparks along the weapon's barrel, and it fires a big blast of ion energy. It washes over the three Jedi ships. The ships shudder, and their lights flicker then go dark.

The *Malevolence* opens fire on two of the ships and destroys them. A shadow falls over Plo Koon's ship as the *Malevolence* draws near.

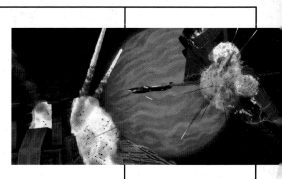

"Quickly, into the pods!" shouts Plo Koon. Plo, Wolffe, and two troopers, Sinker and Boost, scramble into a life pod just before their ship explodes.

"Another successful test. Wouldn't you say Count?" Grievous gloats.

"We must keep our position secret. Send out the hunters. I want all of those life pods destroyed," Count Dooku replies coldly.

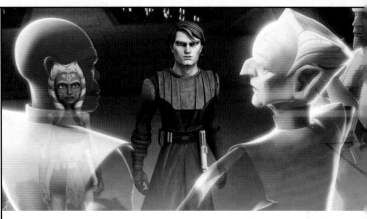

No survivors
All the survivors of the secret weapon have been killed by the Separatists so that there are no witnesses.

Convoy
A convoy is a group of vehicles that travel together so they don't get attacked.

On the *Resolute*, Anakin contacts the Jedi Council on Coruscant over the HoloNet and tells them that he is preparing a rescue mission. The Council thinks it is a bad idea as the Separatists have left no survivors in previous attacks. They tell Anakin that he can't help Plo Koon.

"Wait! Just because there haven't been any survivors before doesn't mean there won't be any this time!" Ahsoka interrupts.

"Excuse my Padawan, we will deploy as you have instructed, Master," Anakin says, turning off the holoprojector.

"Ahsoka!" scolds Anakin.

Obi-Wan Kenobi
Obi-Wan is a Jedi elder and a member of the Jedi Council.

"If anyone could survive, Master Plo could! I don't understand why—"

"What you don't understand is Jedi protocol. Or your place, my young Padawan," Anakin says.

Jedi protocol
Jedi must follow the decisions of the Jedi Council, even if they disagree with them.

Commander Wolffe
Commander Wolffe serves on board the *Triumphant*.

Life pod
A life pod is a small craft that launches from a ship that has been destroyed, in order to save those inside.

Plo and the clones look around them. The explosion has burnt out all the power to the life pod. They set to work trying to restore it. Commander Wolffe spots another pod in space. Plo uses the Force to turn the pod around. It's been cut open and the clone troopers inside are dead. Plo Koon and the clones realize that they are in great danger. Anakin and Ahsoka get on board a smaller ship, the

Twilight, which is in the hangar of the *Resolute* and launch into space.

"Master, I should tell you why I spoke up before…" Ahsoka begins.

"You don't have to explain anything," Anakin replies.

Ahsoka realizes that Anakin is going to go on a rescue mission.

"So it's okay when you don't follow what the Council says," Ahsoka says angrily.

"Doing what the Jedi Council says, that's one thing; how we go about it, that's another. That's what I'm trying to teach you, my young Padawan," Anakin says.

The Force
The Force is the energy that connects all living things. The Jedi tap into its immense power to perform incredible tasks.

Rocket Battle Droids
Rocket Battle Droids are equipped with rockets to help them to fly in space.

Jedi Temple
All Jedi train from a very young age in the Jedi Temple on the planet Coruscant.

Suddenly, Plo Koon hears a trooper's voice over the life pod's radio.

"This is pod one-nine-seven-seven. We are under attack! Is anyone out there?"

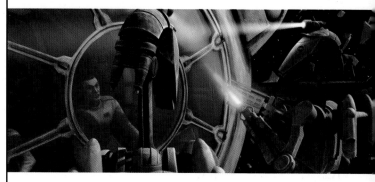

The boarding ship flies up and locks onto the other life pod. Four Rocket Battle Droids float over. Plo watches the nearby pod helplessly as they break in and kill the clone troopers inside.

Meanwhile, Anakin is still searching for Plo Koon. Anakin asks Ahsoka how she knows Plo Koon.

"He's one of my oldest friends. It was Master Plo Koon who found me and brought me to the temple, where I belonged. Now he's lost, so I thought… maybe I could find him."

The radio buzzes. It's Obi-Wan.

"Oh, hello Master. Uh, we made a quick stop in the Abregado system," Anakin says.

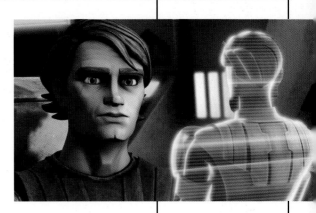

"A rescue mission, I suppose? You had other orders," scolds Obi-Wan.

Ahsoka pipes up. "It was my idea, Master Obi-Wan."

"Oh, I'm sure. Well, have you found any survivors?" asks Obi-Wan. "No, you were right. The Separatists don't want any witnesses," Anakin replies. They are about to give up their search when Anakin's droid, R2-D2, picks up a signal.

Abregado system
The Abregado system is situated in the Core Worlds region. It has a reputation as a rough area.

Useful droid
One of R2-D2's many uses is to scan space for any signs of life, mechanical, electrical, or natural.

The Jedi
Jedi are a diplomatic, peace-keeping force. In this time of war, they have sworn to protect the Republic.

Viewport
A viewport is a window that looks out into space.

The Rocket Battle Droids will attack Plo Koon's life pod next.

"It is time to go," Plo Koon says.

"Go? Where are you going, sir?" asks Commander Wolffe.

"Outside to destroy the enemy. I can withstand the pressure for a brief time. Put your helmets on."

The boarding ship attaches and the Battle Droids start cutting into the viewport. One of the Battle Droids looks up and sees…

Plo Koon, Sinker, and Boost standing on top of the pod.

"Hey what's a Jedi doing out here?" the Battle Droid asks, confused.

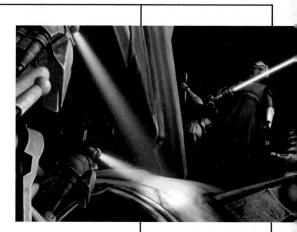

Plo cuts the Battle Droid's head off with his lightsaber. The clones open fire. The Battle Droids dart behind the ship. The pincers on the boarding ship start to squeeze the pod, crushing it inward, with Wolffe still inside.

Plo uses the Force to push Sinker into range and he fires

Lightsaber
A lightsaber can cut through almost any material.

on the Battle Droids, destroying them. Plo Koon swipes his blade through the pincer blades and frees the pod.

Chancellor Palpatine
Chancellor Palpatine is the head of the Republic's government. He often sits in on Jedi Council meetings to help decide on important issues.

Obi-Wan reports Anakin's disobedience to the Jedi Council back on Coruscant. Chancellor Palpatine orders Anakin back to his post straight away. Even though R2-D2 picked up Plo Koon's life pod signal, Anakin and Ahsoka must follow orders and turn back.

"I know he's alive! I can sense it!" Ahsoka says excitedly, grabbing the controls of the *Twilight*.

Plo Koon and the clone troopers have nearly given up hope when suddenly they are illuminated by a brilliant light. It's the *Twilight*!

Ahsoka winches in Plo's life pod with a tow harpoon and cable.

"Are you okay, Master Plo?" asks Ahsoka. Plo Koon's alien breathers work overtime to breathe.

"Were there any survivors?" Plo asks.

"We couldn't find anybody else," replies Anakin sadly.

"The hunters must have destroyed the rest."
"I'm sorry, Master Plo," Ahsoka says.

Tow harpoon and cable
A harpoon shoots out a hook attached to a cable. It hook onto something which can then be pulled in.

Breathers
Not all aliens breathe air. Plo Koon is a Kel Dor from Dorin and has a mask to turn air into a gas that he can breathe.

"We tracked the mystery weapon to this system. That is when we found out it was an ion cannon," Plo Koon informs Anakin and Ahsoka.

"An ion cannon?" Ahsoka asks.

"A weapon that neutralizes all power to our ships, leaving the targets defenseless," Plo explains.

Suddenly, the *Twilight*'s scanners start to beep.

"Shut down the power system before they detect us!" Plo Koon warns.

Plo starts to switch everything off. He tells Ahsoka to turn off R2-D2 as well.

"Sorry, little guy," Ahsoka tells R2-D2.

R2-D2
R2-D2 is an astromech droid that helps Anakin to fly spaceships.

The *Malevolence* cruises past.
Grievous and Dooku look out
onto the field of debris.

"There is still no signal from the
pod hunter," says a Battle Droid.

"Reduce speed and activate your
scanners. We will find who is
responsible," Grievous says.

A Battle Droid pinpoints the
Twilight's position. The
Malevolence turns. It's
coming back to attack!

Ion cannon
The Separatist
ion cannon
shoots out a
wave of ion
energy that
acts like a
power cut to all
the machines
it hits.

"They're coming back!" Anakin realizes.

The door opens and a medical droid enters the cockpit.

"We forgot to shut off the medical droid," Ahsoka says.

"We've got to get the power back on now!" shouts Anakin. Anakin and Ahsoka prepare the ship to make their escape.

The *Twilight* weaves its way through the debris of the earlier attack on the Jedi Cruisers.

"Target range almost locked, sir," says one of Grievous's Battle Droids.

"They're not going to make it," Grievous sneers.

Medical droid
A medical droid is programmed to give medical treatment.

"Artoo, program the hyperdrive!" Ahsoka commands, after Plo has switched him back on again.

Meanwhile, the *Malevolence* has the *Twilight* in its targets. Grievous gives the command to fire!

But they are too late as Anakin expertly pilots the ship out through the last pieces of debris and they surge out into open space! The tiny ship jumps into hyperspace, leaving the *Malevolence* far behind.

Hyperdrive
A hyperdrive allows spacecraft to travel at lightspeed across huge distances in hyperspace.

Sith Master
General Grievous takes his orders from Count Dooku.

Sith Lord
Dooku's Master is the Sith Lord, Darth Sidious. This shadowy figure rarely shows his face.

"Now the Republic will learn of our secret weapon," General Grievous says angrily.

"Your failure is most unfortunate. I will have to discuss this with my Master," replies Count Dooku coolly.

On the *Twilight*, Wolffe thanks Anakin.

"Thanks for getting us out of there in one piece, General Skywalker."

"You have my Padawan to thank for that," replies Anakin.

"Skywalker, it is time to give our report to the Council," Plo Koon says.

"Come on, Ahsoka," Anakin says.

"You want me there?" Ahsoka lowers her head "I figured because of before…"

Anakin raises her chin tenderly.

"Ahsoka, through it all you never gave up. You did a great job… But if I'm getting in trouble for this, you're gonna share some of the blame, too. So, come on."

"Right beside ya, Skyguy," Ahsoka replies.

They walk off through the busy hangar, a team, with a beeping R2-D2 following.

"Skyguy"
This is Ahsoka's nickname for Anakin. Anakin's nickname for Ahsoka is "Snips" as she was snippy with him when they first met.

Cloak of Darkness

Viceroy Nute Gunray, a scheming Neimoidian, is under arrest. The Jedi Council has assigned Jedi Master Luminara Unduli and Padawan Ahsoka Tano, with the help of clone Commander Gree, to take him to the planet Coruscant. Nute Gunray will stand trial for his war crimes against the Republic. Luminara and Ahsoka must be cautious, as the Separatists will try to rescue him.

The prisoner and his guards arrive on the Republic ship *Tranquillity*, and meet Captain Argyus, the captain of the ship. Nute whispers to Commander Gree.

"Help me get out of here, Commander. I am a man of great wealth, and I can be very generous to my allies."

"That's a very tempting offer, Viceroy. In the meantime, I have a gift for you," replies Gree, slapping a pair of binder cuffs on him.

Bribery
Nute Gunray often tries to bribe his way out of trouble.

Binder cuffs
Binder cuffs go around a criminal's wrists to stop them from escaping.

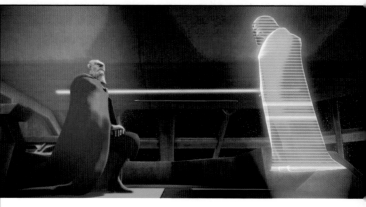

Nute Gunray
Nute Gunray is one of the leaders of the Confederacy of Independent Systems, an important and wealthy individual.

Meanwhile in a Separatist ship, Count Dooku is talking to a hologram of his Master, the mysterious Darth Sidious.

"Gunray's capture could be a serious threat to us, my friend. The Viceroy will not last long under Jedi interrogation," Darth Sidious says.

"I already put a plan into action, my Lord. My best agent, Asajj Ventress, will infiltrate the Jedi ship and either free Gunray or silence him," Count Dooku replies.

A look of concern crosses Darth Sidious's face. Asajj has let them down in the past.

"She is a gifted assassin. You have my word, she will

complete her mission to the letter," assures Count Dooku.

Back on the *Tranquillity*, Luminara probes Nute Gunray's mind with the Force, but he won't tell her any of the Separatists' secrets.

"I am an innocent pawn in all of this!" he proclaims.

Ahsoka has had enough of Nute's whining and ignites her lightsaber and holds it at Nute's throat.

"Tell us what we want to know right now, or I will gut you like a Rokarian dirt fish!" she shouts. Luminara is shocked at Ahsoka's outburst and tells her off.

Asajj Ventress
A deadly assassin trained by Count Dooku, Asajj often takes on dangerous missions to kill Jedi.

Suddenly the ship is rocked by a powerful laser blast. Droid fighters and Separatist boarding ships attack the *Tranquillity*. The boarding ships "stab" the Jedi Cruiser, the ships' sharp pincers split open the cruiser's hull, and droids pour onto the ship.

"Super Battle Droids have breached our hull," informs a clone trooper. "They're heading for the detention level!"

Super Battle Droid
A Super Battle Droid is an upgraded Battle Droid, with reinforced armor plating and inbuilt weaponry.

Luminara and Gree head toward the hull, leaving Ahsoka to guard Nute Gunray.

"It appears you are in no position to negotiate after all, Padawan. Perhaps after my rescue…" Nute Gunray taunts Ahsoka.

"Rescue? Maybe they're here to make sure you won't talk," Ahsoka says.

On a lower deck, Asajj Ventress crawls out of an empty boarding ship. A clone trooper sees her and Ventress severs his head with her two lightsabers. Ventress cuts a hole in an air duct and leaps inside. She activates the comlink on the dead clone's gauntlet and disappears down the duct.

Comlink
A comlink allows people to talk to each other, when they are apart.

31

Commander Gree
Formally known as CC-1004, Commander Gree normally serves with Yoda in the 41st Elite Corps troops.

In the hull, clones are fighting the Super Battle Droids. One of the droids is hit by blaster fire and explodes. The remaining droids look behind them to see Commander Gree and Luminara. Luminara wades into the droids, slashing them with her lightsaber.

Asajj kicks her way out of the air duct into the reactor room. A small droid swivels around alerted by the noise. "Who is there?" it asks. Ventress hides from the droid, unseen. Two clone troopers enter the room.

"See anything?" asks one of the clones to the droid.

The droid is not sure and continues its search. Ventress crouches like a spider on the ceiling out of view.

"You keep watch here, Threetwentyseven," one of them says.

The droid beeps, annoyed.

"Okay, okay, Threetwentyseven-Tee," says the clone.

"You know droids never like to be called by their nicknames," reminds the other one, as they leave the room.

Ventress sticks some thermal detonators on to the power cores and silently darts back up the air duct.

Thermal detonators
These are powerful bombs that explode and create fires.

Power cores
Where a ship gets its energy to fly from.

327-T
This Treadwell Droid is primarily responsible for maintenance.

Meanwhile, Commander Gree and Luminara destroy the remaining droids. On the detention block, Ventress suddenly drops in from the ceiling and kicks away two guards.

"If it isn't the hairless harpy!" Ahsoka says, recognizing Ventress.

"If it isn't Skywalker's filthy little pet," Ventress answers. "Stand down and I'll give you a cookie."

"How nice of you! Tell you what: I'll give you a merciful death," Ahsoka replies.

Previous battles
Ahsoka has battled Ventress before. She and Anakin rescued the kidnapped Rotta the Huttlet from the Separatists.

In the hull,
Luminara senses
Ventress's presence
and rushes to help.
Captain Argyus
shoots twice at Ventress but she
deflects his blasts and Force-lifts
him up, smashing him into the
ceiling. She uses the
Force to open the door
to Nute Gunray's cell. Ahsoka
charges into Ventress, but she steps
aside and kicks Ahsoka into the
cell. Nute Gunray slips out and
the door slams shut.

"How do you like your room
now?" taunts Nute Gunray.

Jedi sense
Jedi can often
sense someone's
presence, when
they are
approaching
or they can't
see them.

Turbo-lift
A turbo-lift is very fast as it is powered by a turbo.

The turbo-lift doors swish open and out runs Luminara.

"Halt assassin!" she shouts.

As she runs toward Ventress, Luminara uses the Force to open the cell door, freeing Ahsoka. Ahsoka rushes out and attacks Ventress with Luminara. They have her boxed in.

Remote device
When pressed, a remote device can set off a bomb from a distance.

"Surrender," commands Luminara. Ventress lowers her blades and switches them off. Unseen, she presses a button on a remote device. BOOM!

Explosions rock the reactor room, where Ventress had planted the thermal detonators.

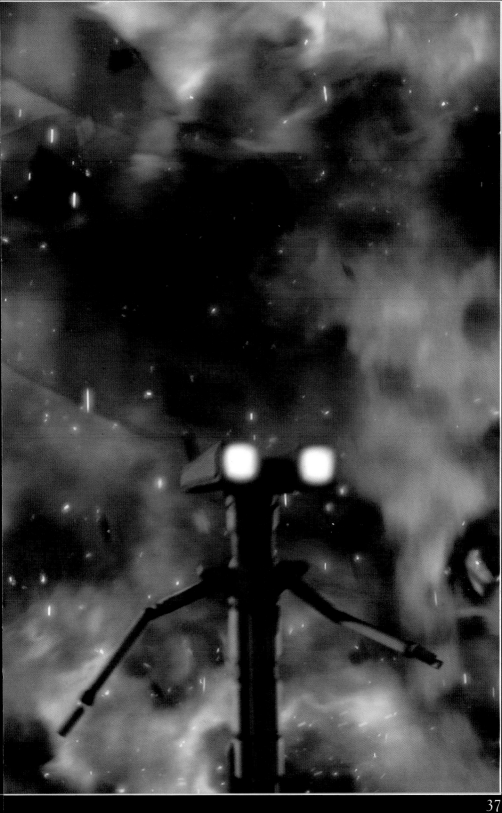

Ventress seizes her chance to escape, and flips away down the corridor. She opens the turbo-lift doors and jumps down the lift shaft. Luminara and Ahsoka run toward the lift door.

Acrobat assassin
Ventress is very athletic and can somersault out of the line of fire.

Ahsoka is about to jump down the lift shaft after Ventress, but Luminara pulls her back—just as a turbo-lift flashes past!

"Our attacker has come for Gunray. Stay here and guard him. I'll confront her myself," Luminara tells Ahsoka.

"Master, with all due respect, Ventress is too powerful for any one Jedi to fight alone. Let me help you," replies Ahsoka.

"I am more than capable of dealing with a lone assassin armed with undisciplined fighting skills," Luminara says haughtily. "Stay here and keep a clear head."

Luminara Unduli
Luminara is a Jedi from the planet Mirial. She is a stickler for the rules and likes to do everything by-the-book.

Ventress flees to the reactor room where she planted the bombs earlier. Luminara follows her into the room, and Ventress attacks! Luminara jumps out of the way but Ventress slashes through a pipe, sending a jet of scalding steam into Luminara's face. Luminara screams.

Ahsoka is on the detention block with Captain Argyus, guarding Nute Gunray who is back in his cell.

"I can't let her face that lowlife alone." Ahsoka says

"Sometimes being a good soldier means doing what you think is

Ventress's past
As a child, Ventress was trained as a Jedi on her homeworld of Rattatak by Jedi Knight Ky Narec, but turned to the dark side when he was killed.

right," replies Argyus. Ahsoka decides to abandon her post and leaves Argyus guarding Nute Gunray.

Luminara rubs her stinging eyes, she can hardly defend herself against Ventress's vicious attacks.

"Even with my vision clouded, I recognize the style of Count Dooku," says Luminara. "Your version is unrefined. Amateurish. Sloppy."

Ventress attacks Luminara in a savage fury, pushing her off a ledge.

"Now you fall as all Jedi must," Ventress sneers.

Captain Argyus
He is a high-ranking Senate Commando and Captain of the *Tranquillity*.

Secret messages
By sending a red signal light, Ventress instructs someone else on the ship to make their move, as agreed.

Suddenly Ventress is pushed out of the air and smashes into a wall. Behind her stands Ahsoka. Ahoska frees Luminara from a pipe which is pinning her down.

"I know, I know… you told me to stay!" Ahsoka says to Luminara.

"Well, as long as you're here, you can help out," Luminara smiles.

Luminara and Ahsoka fight Ventress, but she leaps away and out of their sight. She presses a button on her gauntlet turning on a red light.

A red light flashes on Captain Argyus's gauntlet. Argyus draws his blaster and shoots the guards. Down the corridor, Gree saw what happened and realizes something is wrong. He shoots at Argyus, but misses. Argyus fires back as he pulls Gunray from his cell.

"No, please don't…" pleads Gunray.

"Oh, do shut up. Count Dooku is paying me a fortune to deliver your slimy carcass, so please try to stay alive," snaps Argyus.

The Jedi have lost Ventress. Luminara apologizes to Ahsoka for not listening to her earlier. Just then Luminara's comlink buzzes.

"General Unduli! We've been betrayed! Argyus has freed Gunray!" Gree says.

Jedi tandem fighting
Because Jedi use the Force, they are particularly good at fighting together as a pair. Each knows the movements that the other will make before they make them.

Clones
The Republic bred the clone troopers as an elite fighting force to make up its army. They were all cloned from one man; a bounty hunter called Jango Fett.

Argyus pushes Nute Gunray down the corridor, using him as a shield.

"Stop! This is your last warning!" Commander Gree shouts.

Argyus shoves Gunray into Gree, knocking the blaster from Gree's hand to the floor.

"Why'd you do it, Argyus?"

"I want a life with more than empty servitude," replies Argyus.

"And for that you'd betray the Republic?" Gree asks.

"Like I told the Padawan: Sometimes being a good soldier means doing what you think is right," Argyus explains.

"You and I disagree on what makes a good soldier," Gree says, grabbing the gun and pointing it at Argyus.

Gree is knocked out from behind by Nute Gunray. Argyus presses a green button on his gauntlet.

Ventress's gauntlet flashes green. She pulls out a detonator and tosses it into an air-shaft. She leaps into the shaft as the force of the explosion pushes her upward. She escapes from the Jedi.

With the *Tranquillity* still in turmoil, Nute Gunray and Captain Argyus take a ship unnoticed. Ventress also escapes in a life pod.

Prison break
By knocking out Gree and shooting the other guards, Nute Gunray and Captain Argyus are free to escape.

Betrayal
This is not the first time that someone has betrayed the Republic. R3-S6, R2-D2's replacement, was programmed to sabotage Anakin and Ahsoka's mission—until R2-D2 dealt with him!

"As successful a rescue as one could hope for, Viceroy. I'll be a legend for this," Argyus brags.

The bridge door opens and Ventress strides in.

"I will, of course, make sure your contributions are noted in my report to Count Dooku," says Argyus to Ventress.

Ventress follows the plan earlier agreed upon with her Master and she stabs Argyus through the back of the chair.

"I'll tell him myself," she snarls.

Ahsoka and Luminara give their report of events to Yoda and Anakin. The Jedi realize they can track the stolen ship and they make plans to follow it.

"I owe you my life, Ahsoka," says Luminara.

"Protecting a Jedi Master is the role of a Padawan," Ahsoka says.

"And teaching is usually the role of the Master. Master Skywalker should be proud," Luminara replies.

"Thank you, Master," Ahsoka says gratefully.

Tracking
The ship that Nute Gunray and Captain Argyus stole was fitted with a tracking device. This means that it can be followed by the Jedi wherever it goes.

Glossary

amateurish
Not skilful or
competent.

carcass
A dead body.

combination
Two or more things
mixed together.

communicate
To talk or converse
with someone else.

debris
Rubbish that is left
after an explosion or
demolition.

deploy
To send into action.

diplomatic
Of diplomats or
international
relations.

disobedience
Refusing to obey
commands.

flagship
The ship that carries
the commander of
a fleet.

illuminated
Lit up by a
bright light.

immense
Very large.

infiltrate
To enter something
gradually or
unobtrusively,
often to spy on it.

internal
On the inside of
something.

interrogate
To question formally,
exhaustively or
aggressively.

malevolence
The intention to do
harm to others.

merciful
Showing mercy
or compassion for
someone else.

negotiate
To attempt to come
to a compromise
using dialog.

neutralize
To make neutral
by counteracting
the effect of
something.

position
Where something is.

probe
To investigate in a
penetrating way.

protocol
A system of conduct
that is carried out on
official occasions.

reinforce
To strengthen
something, using extra
forces or material.

revolving
Going around in
a circle.

sabotage
To purposely destroy
something, using
devious methods.

servitude
Serving someone
or something else.

silhouette
A shadow around the
shape of something,
on a light background.

surging
Moving ahead quickly.

triumphant
Victorious or
successful.